Old Gardenstown

CW00404305

with Crovie and Pennan

Kay Beaton

DEN OF AFFORSK GAMRIE.

This view of the villages of Gardenstown and Crovie (pronounced 'Crivie') remains largely unchanged today. The main B9031 road still follows the coast eastwards from Macduff, although at the Den of Afforsk it now takes a slightly different route up out of the den to the one shown here (the route of the original road is still visible today). The cottage on the left was once home to Henry Birnie, who suffered from tuberculosis as a child, and his spinster sister, Annie. They had a loom in one of the outhouses where they ran a small business weaving and knitting socks. Today the cottage is a ruin. The narrower track in the centre of the photograph leads to St John's Church. The conical hill in the middle is Castle Hill, the site of an ancient motte and bailey fortification which was a wooden or stone keep built on a raised earthwork called a motte, with an enclosed courtyard – a bailey. Local tradition says the castle belonged to the son of Hamelyn de Troup. In 1308 this castle, together with those of Cullykhan and Dundarg along the coast, were destroyed in the 'harrying of Buchan' by Robert the Bruce.

1

Text © Kay Beaton, 2012.
First published in the United Kingdom, 2012,
by Stenlake Publishing Ltd.
Telephone: 01290 551122
www.stenlake.co.uk

ISBN 9781840336092

The publishers regret that they cannot supply copies of any pictures featured in this book.

Acknowledgements

I would like to thank everyone who helped with contributions to this book: Eleanor and John Hepburn, Sue Scarrott, Gamrie Heritage Centre for use of a selection of photographs from their extensive collection, John O'Neill for keeping me right with historical details, the residents of Gardenstown for providing a wealth of information about the photographs, the village and the local area, the assistants in various local libraries, and my partner David for his support and patience.

Picture Acknowledgements

The publishers wish to thank Margaret and Michael Henry who generously contributed all of the photographs in this book except for those listed below.

The author wishes to thank Gamrie Heritage Centre for contributing the photographs on pages 2, 7, 18, 20, 25, 26, 27, 33 and 44.

Left: William Murray started his first bakery at 108 Main Street in the 1890s before the business moved to these premises on Bankhead, Main Street, in 1920. The small lean-to building behind the group housed the engine which drove the bakehouse machinery. The engine was started every morning at 4.00 a.m. The business moved again into purpose-built bakehouse premises on Main Street in the mid 1930s, and opened the shop across the street at No. 96. Murray's was one of the oldest established bakers in the area and after 120 years of baking sadly closed its doors in April 2011. The old bakery building on the Bankhead was later used by Tommy Watt, a joiner and ironmonger.

Introduction

Gardenstown, or Gamrie as it is known locally, is the largest of three fishing villages situated on Gamrie Bay, the other two being Crovie and Pennan. The Parish of Gamrie, in which Gardenstown and Crovie are located, is approximately ten miles long by three miles wide. It is bordered to the north by the Moray Firth, on the east by the Parish of Aberdour, to the south by the parishes of Monquhitter and King Edward, and on the west by the River Deveron.

After the 1715 Jacobite Rebellion the government made money available to local lairds for the building of bridges and harbours in their communities in an effort to prevent conditions that would lead to further rebellions. Using these funds, the community of Powieston was developed by the local laird, Alexander Garden of Troup, primarily as a fishing village to encourage the catching of white fish, and it was officially renamed as Gardenstown in 1720. The lucrative herring fishing industry proved to be beneficial as it provided employment and also encouraged shopkeepers and tradesmen into the village to serve the growing local population.

Along from Gardenstown, on the east coast of Gamrie Bay, is the tiny village of Crovie, a single row of houses built between the seawall and the cliffs. During the village's heyday Crovie had its own shop, a meeting hall and even a bakehouse, but Gardenstown grew at Crovie's expense after the great storm of 31 January 1953. This washed away the path between the villages, together with stretches of Crovie's sea defences, and a number of houses and sheds. Crovie ceased to be viable almost immediately, and many residents sold their houses for virtually nothing in the rush to move to Gardenstown; it is recorded that one man sold his house for £10! Nowadays, Crovie is home to only a couple of families and most of the houses are used as holiday homes.

Besides fishing, the area has also depended on agriculture and the land surrounding the villages has been farmed for hundreds of years. It was not natural agricultural land, being very hilly, but there were some areas of good soil and due to sheer hard work and efficient crop husbandry it was greatly improved. The staple crops of potatoes and turnips were introduced into the area by the Gamrie parish minister, Mr Wilson, in the mid 1700s, and advancements in agricultural techniques and the introduction of new farm machinery in the early part of the nineteenth century, such as swing ploughs, iron-toothed harrows and wheeled carts, made farming the land a lot easier.

The villagers of the parish have always been well catered for spiritually and, at one point, the community had as many as eight places of worship: the village Kirk on The Green, the parish church which is one mile out of the village, five meeting halls in Gardenstown, and one in Crovie. To the west of the village, and visible from most parts of Gardenstown, are the remains of the Church of St John the Evangelist. This predates the village, being built in 1513, and replaced an earlier church of 1004 which had been built to celebrate the defeat of the Danes at the Battle of the Bloody Pits (or 'Bleedy Pots').

In 1004, after being defeated at the Battle of Aberlemno in Angus, the Danes retreated to their ships and headed for Caithness. The weather was against them and they were forced to take shelter in Gamrie Bay. A raiding party of about 600 men was put ashore on the 'Braid Sands' and they moved inland where they rounded up cattle and other farm animals and began to drive them back to the shore. As they re-entered the Den of Afforsk they saw that the Scottish army, under the command of Mermane Mormaer of Buchan, had taken up position on Castle Hill, overlooking the point where they intended to re-embark.

Abandoning their original plan to get back to their ships, the Danes moved out along Mohr Head. They remained there hoping that the Scots would be drawn down from their strong position to one where they could be defeated. But the Scots were reluctant to attack these fierce Norse warriors; Mormaer decided to appeal for 'Divine help' and declared to his army that if they were to defeat the Danes he would build a Church to St John on the very site where the enemy was encamped.

Half of the Scottish army moved round to the top of Mohr Head into a position above the Danes, and there they threw stones down on them while the other half launched an attack across the Den of Afforsk, forcing the Danes to the top of Mohr Head. Meanwhile, their comrades on the ships set sail westwards to Greenside, near the Mill of Cullen, and landed more men in an effort to help their countrymen.

Back at the battle, having reached the top of Mohr Head, the Danes took up a defensive position. The battle moved back and forth, and being joined by the second party, they eventually succeeded in driving the Scots back down the hill. However, Scottish numbers were increasing all the time as more reinforcements began to arrive after seeing the series of fires being lit on high mounds across this and neighbouring parishes. Once again they advanced on the Danes and drove them back up the hill, until they had them cornered at the point of Mohr Head. The Scottish army succeeded in trapping them as the steep cliffs behind the Danes made withdrawal impossible and all were massacred. After the battle the bodies of the dead Danes were thrown into the many natural hollows or pits in the ground nearby. These open graves were named the 'Bloody Pits', by which they are still known.

The promise made by Mormaer of Buchan was kept and a small church was built on the site of the Danish camp. The skulls of three of the Danish chiefs were built into an alcove in one of the walls, where they remained until the building fell into a neglected ruin in the 1950s. Two of the skulls were stolen but the third is now on public display in the museum in Banff Library.

By the 1920s Gardenstown and Crovie together housed around 250 fishermen and fifty fishing boats. This number declined over the following years in the face of competition from the larger and more effective vessels that could operate from other ports such as Macduff and Fraserburgh. Competition from larger supermarkets in nearby towns has had a detrimental effect on the economy of Gardenstown and in April 2011 a double blow was dealt to the village. Murray Brother's bakers, whose family had been baking in the village since the 1890s, closed its doors for the last time on the retirement of Bill and Douglas Murray. The butcher next door, William Fraser & Son, who had also relied upon the baker's ovens to bake pies, also closed after thirty years in the village. There are still a few long established businesses remaining, such as the eighteenth-century Garden Arms which is one of the oldest buildings in the village. Some newer small businesses have more recently sprung up to accommodate the local and growing tourist trade.

The village of Pennan lies four miles east of Gardenstown in the Parish of Aberdour which is approximately seven miles wide by eleven miles long. It is bordered to the north by the Moray Firth, on the east by the parishes of Pitsligo, Tyrie, Fraserburgh and Strichen, to the south by New Pitsligo, New Deer and King Edward, and on the west by the Parish of Gamrie, the boundary of which is marked by the burn of Nethermill. Pennan was founded in 1780 as a fishing village. Like Crovie, most of Pennan's native families have moved away and many of the houses are now used as holiday homes. Pennan leapt to fame in 1983 after its starring role as the fictional village of Ferness in the Bill Forsyth film *Local Hero*. The red phone box, made famous by the film, sits directly opposite the Pennan Inn. Attempts to have the phone box removed were met with public outcry which led to it being listed by Historic Scotland in 1989. The village made it into the headlines again in 2003, when the then owner of the Pennan Inn painted the exterior of the building aqua blue. The Scottish Executive had to step in and order the owner to repaint it white.

The trio of picturesque villages has attracted a number of film and TV crews over the years. Besides *Local Hero*, the area's film credits include the 1992 film *Salt On Our Skin* starring Greta Scacchi, the critically acclaimed John MacKay short film *Doom and Gloom*, the 2007 reality TV programme *The Baron* in which Malcolm McLaren, Mike Reid and Suzanne Shaw all competed for the title 'Baron of Troup', the 2009 Morrison's 'Fresh Fish' advert starring Robert Lindsay and the 2010 BBC Four documentary *Shanties and Sea Songs*.

Note on 'by names' or 'tee names' used in this book: In the villages along the Moray Firth coast it was common for individuals to be given 'by names' or 'tee names' to distinguish them from other persons who had the same surname. Where a 'tee name' for a person is known it appears in brackets after their name.

KIRKYARD, GAMRIE - CHURCH ERECTED 1004.

On the hillside to the west of Gardenstown stands the ruins of the Church of St John the Evangelist. This church was used by the whole parish of Gamrie, which at the time also included Macduff. In the spring of 1827, after the building had fallen into ruin, it was decided that services would be held in the churchyard during the summer and in the old School of Findon and the Society Hall in Gardenstown during the winter. It was replaced in 1830 by the new parish church, which was built a mile inland. In the churchyard seen here there are approximately 310 tombstones, some dating as far back as the sixteenth century. The last person to be buried here was Barbara Ingram, who died on 1 September 1952, aged ninety. Due to the steepness of the roads surrounding the area, coffins were transported by boat along the coast and hoisted up the cliff face.

SWALLOW ROCK & GARDENSTOWN.

27.

Swallow Rock got its name due to swallows taking advantage of the little nooks and crannies in the sandstone cliffs in which they built their nests. At this point in the cliffs there are two shallow sea caves. The cliffs in the foreground, which are to the west of the village, are of old red sandstone topped by glacial deposits from the last ice age. This seam of old red sandstone runs inland for approximately 21 miles, to just south of Fyvie, and in width from Gardenstown to the Red Head at Pennan. Behind the position of the photographer is the major geological junction between the younger old red sandstone and the much older metamorphic rocks where a harder quartzite can be found. The 'Old Red' of Gamrie is famous for the fossil fish which have been found there.

This is the wreck of the *Betty of Malmo* on the beach at Gardenstown. On 17 November 1893 a massive storm, reported in the *Banffshire Journal* as being 'the worst for more than forty years', struck the northeast coast of Scotland. A number of ships were driven ashore at Findhorn, Burghead, Banff and Gardenstown. *Betty*, a three-masted schooner from the Swedish port of Malmo, was on her way to Inverness with coal from Grangemouth when she ran aground in Gamrie Bay. High winds and blinding sleet hampered the rescue attempt and it was several hours before the coastguard could get a line to the ship and bring the crew safely ashore. They attached a breeches buoy around the houses at the highest point of the Seatown, known as the 'cassa' or causeway, and pulled the crew through the waves to this point. The ship's dog however, waited until the tide went out and walked up the beach completely dry! The coal was bought by 'The Receiver of Wrecks' and given to the villagers and is said to have kept Gamrie's fires burning for more than a year.

Gardenstown is the largest of the three fishing villages situated on Gamrie Bay, the other two being Crovie and Pennan. In the past Gardenstown had also been known as Powieston and the Shore of Gamrie. According to tradition the name Gamrie comes from the Gaelic word 'Kemrie' meaning a 'running leap' or 'running fight' owing to the Battle of the Bloody Pits. At the bottom right of this photograph you can see where the old Seatown road slopes down towards the level of the beach at the end. Before the days of proper sanitation, there would have been a midden on the beach at the bottom of each close where household waste and the contents of the 'pail' (a chamber pot) from the glory-hole would have been disposed of. The first house in Gardenstown to have an indoor toilet and bath was that of James Nicol – merchant at 55 Seatown. You can also just make out the sewage pipe on the beach in front of the house at the end of Seatown, and the four children who are playing on it!

GARDENSTOWN.

The oldest part of the village, Seatown, is located along Gamrie Bay and around the harbour area. The houses were built on a series of terraces cut into the hillside with nothing but a narrow road separating the houses from the water. They were constructed gable-end onto the sea to provide maximum protection from the cold northerly winds. The road down to Seatown descends about 500 feet in a little over a mile, via a series of sharp hairpin bends. The steepness of this incline means that anyone using the road is practically looking down the chimney pots of the houses below. The area behind, where the children are sitting, was used as a drying green for washing. The flat area in the centre of the photograph is known as the 'Biggin'. This area was built in 1908 as a defence against the sea. In 1910 a series of wooden poles were added as a breakwater to protect the more vulnerable centre part. Originally there would have been twelve poles – in more recent years these have been referred to as the 'Twelve Apostles', with the broken one (which has been damaged by time and tide) named 'Judas'. During the 1950s local children used the poles to play leap frog.

The houses in Seatown were built from either locally quarried red sandstone, taken from the west of the village, or 'blue stone' – the blue-grey slate from nearby quarries. Some of the earlier houses were built using the same method as a dry stone dyke, and the walls are between one and two feet thick with small windows and narrow doorways. The sandstone houses were then harled and whitewashed to help protect them from the elements. Usually consisting of two storeys, a Seatown house has two rooms downstairs, one used as a kitchen and the other as a living/bedroom. Older houses would have a 'butt 'n' ben': a permanent bed which was built into the wall with a storage space underneath. The upper storey, or loft space, was used either to mend and store nets or bait long line hooks. Between the rows of houses there is a network of pathways or 'closes'. The white house at the bottom of the photograph was Maggie Wiseman's house. In front of this, where the shed is, there was once another row of low-roofed houses known as Landing Street. These would have been the most basic of dwellings with dirt floors. The area behind Maggie's house is known as 'The Goose Park'. Before the houses were built there the area was owned by the innkeeper of the Seatown Inn – he had an enclosure there in which he kept geese.

GARDENSTOWN.

As the village continued to expand, space 'down the brae' began to run out and the village started to move up the hill. The first houses to be built at the top of the village were on Craigen Terrace, behind the village hall. The county council built sixteen houses there around 1938, with the two blocks of four flats being the first. At that time Craigen Terrace was known as the 'New Road' and was the main road out of the village. The area to the right of Craigen Terrace, where Garden Crescent is today, was known as the 'Shepherds Lye' and was used to dry fishing nets. The large white house at the top right of this photograph is the Manse and is still used by the minister today. At the end of the 1800s an area of ground to the east of the harbour was reclaimed from the sea and a new sea wall was built to protect it – this area is known as the 'Newground'. The two cottages at the far lower right were destroyed in the Great Storm of 1953. Between these and the cottage at the end of Seatown can be seen the poles at the 'Biggin'.

Opposite: Sandy Dey inspecting the damage caused to his home by the storm of January 1953. Sandy and his wife Millicent lived in part of the house on the left, while an elderly lady, Jessie Lovie McDonald, lived in the other part. Even with the house in this state, she refused to leave and was eventually carried out and up the cliff in her bed! During the storm, when the Deys saw the waves starting to rise higher they decided to try to blockade the front door using a section of a mast. They wedged it between the back of the door and the stairs but then one particularly strong wave crashed through the door and pushed the staircase right out the back of the house. The house on the right was the home of Barbara and John Hepburn. Much of the weather in January 1953 was unusually mild, being more like late spring than mid winter. Towards the end of the month the temperature fell but there was little indication of what was to come. In the early hours of 31 January hurricane force winds swept down from Iceland over Britain and Holland, causing widespread destruction. These two houses, to the west of the Seatown (and shown in the far lower right of the previous photograph), were completely destroyed and a shop further along Seatown (No. 50) was flooded and had its windows and doors smashed. Seatown itself was protected a little by the 'new' road built on top of the seawall. The earth banks, below Main Street and to the west of the harbour, were undermined. The Newground area was flooded and wooden sheds and garages were damaged and destroyed. Power and telephone cables were blown down and, inland, farmers lost stacks of straw, farm building roofs and livestock. The winds were so strong that 45 gravestones in the churchyard were blown over. The greatest damage however was done to Crovie. The Sneuk footpath was washed away, while sheds, garages and the seawall at the west end were destroyed, together with some of the houses. Others were heavily damaged. After this many of the Crovie residents sold their properties and moved to Gardenstown.

Right: A clearer view of the 'new' Seatown road – journeying along it can still be precarious, but it has protected the houses from further storm damage over the years. At the top right, left of the three wooden garages, stands the village hall, originally built as a volunteer drill hall. It was bought after the First World War by six local businessmen and, in order to guarantee its future, a Hall Committee was formed. Its constitution stipulated that the committee was to include the local councillor, school headmaster, local doctor and the two local bank managers. Additional members would be elected at the AGM. Although some of the positions no longer exist, the committee still functions today. Wedding receptions were held in the village hall and the local baker would have provided the traditional fare of baked yellow fish, steak pie and maybe a trifle or pudding. Saturday night dances were also held, but the most popular dance was on New Year's Day and people would attend from all over the parish. Behind the hall are the two blocks of flats in Craigen Terrace.

GARDENSTOWN.

56002

Below left: Although this picture is labelled 'Strait Path', it's actually a Seatown close known locally as 'Toog's Close' after one of its inhabitants. Toog's proper name was George Alexander Mair. In 1907, the then thirteen-year-old Toog lived with his widowed mother, Mary Mair (nee Watt) in No. 48 (the first door on the left of the photograph). When Toog grew up and married, he moved into the house across the close from his mother, No. 45, and after his mother died he turned her old house into a garage for his car. In 1907, around the time when this photograph was taken, No. 47 (second left) was the home of fisherman George Nicol and his wife, Elizabeth Jane, and their daughter, Jessie Mary. In the three houses across the close from the Nicols lived three brothers, all fishermen, and their wives: in No. 45 (first right) lived William and Margaret Wiseman, in No. 46 was Alexander and Elizabeth Wiseman, and in No. 46a lived James and Barbara Wiseman. The triangular contraption hanging on the wall of No. 46, above the heads of the children on the steps, is called a 'hake' and was used for drying fish.

Above: A group of children and fishermen have gathered outside the soutar's shop at the bottom of Strait Path. The soutar, or cobbler's, name was Sim (Simmie) and he repaired footwear for the whole of the community from children's shoes to fishermens' sea boots. He was also the local postie! This was one of two soutars' shops in the village, the other being on the Main Street. The area here at the bottom of Strait Path is known as the 'cassa' – it was around these houses that the rope for the breeches buoy was tied when saving the crew of the *Betty of Malmo*. It was onto this ledge that the crew were pulled. In the distance the masts in the harbour are those of Fifies, a type of fishing boat that was used around the beginning of the 1900s.

STRAIT PATH GARDENSTOWN

Strait Path is a steep pedestrian path leading up from Seatown to Main Street. The building on the right was the Commercial Bank of Scotland, one of two banks which had branches in the village. This one closed in the 1970s. The first banker here was a Mr Barclay and before it became a bank it was a general merchant's shop owned by Alec Ritchie. Jimmy Scott (Scottie), second from the left on the steps, lived with his family on Denside, the close which runs to the right of the bank. Joseph Watt was also born in a house on Denside in 1887; known as 'VC Joe', he was the only fisherman ever to win the Victoria Cross, awarded for 'extraordinary courage' during the First World War. He became a national hero when, whilst on patrol service in his fishing boat *Gowanlea*, he took on and defeated the Austro-Hungarian cruiser *Novara* in the Strait of Otranto between Italy and Albania. The house facing down the path, No. 86 Main Street, was Archie Grant's butcher's shop. It is thought that the gentleman in the light coloured sweater standing with his hands on his hips is Archie Grant's father.

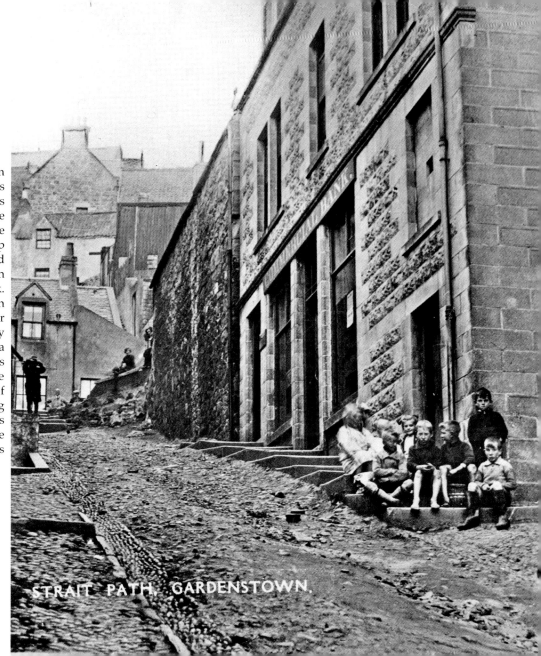

STRAIT PATH, GARDENSTOWN.

The eighteenth-century Garden Arms Hotel is located in the cul-de-sac at the end of Main Street and the top of Strait Path. In 1901 the hotel was run by John Ironside. By 1911 it had changed hands and was run by James Skene. He owned the first motor car in Gardenstown, which arrived in 1912. It was driven by William Birnie who was Skene's driver. The 1911 census tells us that also in residence at the hotel at this time were Meenie Reid, a cook, and Lizzie Shoman, a servant. Could they be two of the women standing on the right of the photograph? The children are sitting at the bottom of the Bankhead.

This is a view of Main Street from the west end. The position of the houses and shops change from that of Seatown, with the broad side of the houses facing north or south. In the early 1900s the horse and cart was still the main form of transport in rural areas and was mainly used by traders. Smaller communities like Gardenstown were dependent upon local shops for provisions. No. 88, to the immediate left, was William Ingram's general merchant's shop and post / telegraph office (the telegraph came to the village in 1878). William lived in the house next door, No. 87, with his wife Margaret and their son, William Sephaskin Ingram. It is believed that the lady in the white blouse is Mrs Ingram and the little boy in the kilt is her son. The next house was owned by Francis Nicol, shoemaker. This and the low house next to it later became the Murrays bakehouse. On the right No. 86 was Grant's butcher's shop although this business later moved across the road to No. 88. No. 90 was the home of William Brown, a tailor who worked out of a building behind No. 87 (the Ingram's house). No. 94 was Alexander Morrison' butcher's shop (indeed, this building has almost always been a butcher's shop). Alexander was also the innkeeper for the Inn in Seatown (No. 49, which is now a private residence). In 1910 the village had four general stores, two butchers, three bakers, four shoemakers, three tailors, two restaurants, two banks, two pubs, one hotel, a boat-building yard and nine fish houses. By 1974 there were four merchants, two with their own bakehouses, a butcher, an ironmonger's shop, a chemist's shop, a shoe shop, a hotel with a pub, and a bank which was only open in the mornings.

Main Street Gardenstown.

A three-wheeled steam lorry parked at the Braehead, Main Street. This lorry is thought to have belonged to the local 'carter' or transport firm, Thompson's of Gardenstown, and helped to maintain vital trade links with the surrounding towns and villages. Pictured are four men preparing to unload the lorry and the two soot-covered men are the drivers! Due to the tight, right-angled turn into the very narrow Main Street, the bags would have been transported along the street on a sack cart – a practice which still continues with every delivery made to the Main Street to this day. During its slow journey up the steep hill, the lorry was often followed by a swarm of children who were fascinated by the great machine.

HIGH STREET, GARDENSTOWN.

Pupils of the Infants' School gather outside on High Street. The entrance to the 'Little Schoolie' was up steps and through a gate next to the house on the far right. It was opened in 1910 to save the little ones the long walk out to Bracoden Public School. They would have attended the school until they were seven; the building is now a Brethren meeting hall. 1875 saw a new era in the schooling of children of Gardenstown and the surrounding area with the opening of Bracoden Public School, one mile out of the village towards Crovie. Bracoden School was to provide education for both girls and boys from five to thirteen years of age.

This was Mrs Sinclair's class of 1925 at the Infant School. Only children from the village of Gardenstown, with the addition of those from The Gardens Farm, attended the school on the High Street. The children from Crovie and the outlying farms went to Bracoden School, which was nearer for them. The 33 children in this photo are, back row (right to left): Mrs Sinclair, George Wiseman, Gilbert West, G. Nicol, Frank West, George Craigen, Willie Dey, Alex Watt, Alex Fraser West, Alex West, Willie Ritchie; middle row (right to left): John Ritchie, Gladys Watt, Olive Watt, Agnes Cunningham Watt, Cathie Watt and her twin Emily Watt, Helen Ritchie, Jeannie Reid West, Isabella Lovie, Ella Wilson, Agnes Nicol, Maggie J. Robertson; front row (right to left): Alex George Alexander, George Watt, Frank Alexander, George Wiseman, James Scott, Jessie Helen Watt, Isabella Wilson, Christian McKay, Ella Wilson, Francis West, Jimmy Dingwall. At the time this picture was taken, the fishing and farming communities were quite separate. Fishermen always chose to marry a girl from a fishing family, someone who understood the way of life and could contribute to the family concern.

The sandy beach to the west of the village has always been a popular playground for the children of the village. Depending upon the tides, the depth of the sand can vary. This uncovers the sandstone bedrock underlying the beach and creates sheltered rock pools which are ideal for sailing toy boats. The Muckle Loch, which is visible when the tide is in, creates a large pool where some of the older villagers remember being taught to swim.

Gardenstown from Craigendargity.

The rock formation on the right of the picture is known as Craigendargity. The Great Storm of January 1953 raised one of the highest tides ever recorded in Gardenstown and during the gale Craigendargity was submerged for two to three hours. Gardenstown Harbour was originally built in 1720, with two stone piers enclosing a triangular tidal basin. It has the reputation of being one of the best strategic positions for a tidal harbour in the Moray Firth, protected from all but the infrequent due north storms.

Below left: The earliest method of fishing employed in the village was using long baited lines from smaller boats, which went out from the harbour daily. The long-line method was used to catch white fish such as ling, cod, haddock, turbot and skate. These lines were approximately 300 feet long; attached to these were shorter lines or 'snoods' which held approximately 150 baited hooks, although the number of hooks on them would vary depending upon the type of fish being caught. All of the hooks would have had to be hand-baited and laid out in a certain way so they could be easily cast at sea, in baskets or 'sculls', like the one the man in the photograph has at his feet. The gathering of the bait – usually mussels, limpets or lug worms – and baiting the hooks was usually done by the fisherman's wife and children. Mussels would have had to be bought, but the lack of money to buy them often meant that the villagers would have had to collect limpets from local shores a few miles away and carry them back in creels, similar to the one the woman has on her back. As well as providing a method for carrying things, such as bait and other general goods, the wicker creels were used for carrying fish for sale.

Above: Around 1900 the herring fleet was made up of sailing boats known as Fifies. Steam vessels were later introduced and a harbour full of sails became an unusual sight. The steam coming from the exhaust on the boat nearest the pier is coming from the capstan. During the eighteenth century the Crown encouraged communities to catch herring for the European market. It wasn't until 1812, however, that drift nets were introduced into the village; that year a local fisherman, William Nicol, was sent to Queensferry for six weeks to learn netting techniques, and with his new found knowledge Gardenstown became one of the first ports in the northeast to fish for herring with nets. By 1839 there were fifteen herring boats and fifteen small line craft fishing out of Gardenstown; almost 60 years later there were 195 fishermen and 92 boats. However, by 1929 the number of boats had been reduced to 48, eighteen of which were steam drifters.

GAMRIE HARBOUR.

The boat on the far right is the steam drifter, BF679 *Fern*. This 87-foot boat was built of wood in 1907 by W. & G. Stephen of Banff for a group of fishermen including Alex Watt and G. Watt of Gardenstown. In 1915 she was requisitioned for war service and, renamed *Fern II*, was utilised as a patrol boat fitted with a three-pounder gun. By 1925 she had been sold again in Aberdeen and was re-registered in Fraserburgh as FR64. In 1931 a group of people from St Combs, Inverallochy and Fraserburgh purchased her and she was renamed *Coral Cluster*. She was scrapped at Peterhead in 1949. The other two larger boats are Fifies. The lighthouse was added at the end of the east pier in 1914.

24

Before the Second World War the fishermen's co-op in Gardenstown employed approximately thirty people. On the far left is the manager, Georgie Watt (Crow). Most of the women wore headscarves, oilskin aprons and wellington boots for protection but the woman in the back row not dressed this way is Norma West who worked in the office. Fish would have been brought into the village from the neighbouring ports of Macduff and Fraserburgh for processing. Herring were gutted and smoked on-site before being boxed and transported throughout Britain.

Dressed in oilskin aprons and wellies, six gutting quines pose in the yard of the fish house at the Newground. From left to right, they are Anna West, Eunice Wiseman, Rosalind Nicol, Ruth Watt, Isobel Watt and Isobel Nicol. During the herring season (May–February) local boats, and indeed gutting quines, would follow the herring from as far north as Lerwick to as far south as Yarmouth and Lowestoft. Young girls were introduced to the job by relatives and friends who would teach them the required skills and also how to fend for themselves. Many of them looked forward to being a gutting quine as it meant a chance to leave home and become financially independent. Strong bonds would often be formed between the girls as they travelled the country and lodged together.

Waiting for the next landing of herring at Scarborough are six gutting quines, all from Gardenstown. Left to right, they are Ruby West (who at this time was fifteen years old), Jessie Webster, Elsie MacLeod, Mary West, Jenny MacLean and Isa Ann Johnston. No time was ever wasted and during quiet times in the curing yards the girls would get their knitting out and produce socks and mittens!

GARDENSTOWN HARBOUR

GN590G

The two skiffs in the foreground here are *Sower*, owned by Benjamin (Mike) Nicol and, next to it, BF319 *Silver Spray*, owned by John George West, who was one of the last full-time fishermen to work out of Gardenstown. Behind them is BF82 *Lustre*, owned by George Nicol and Joseph Alexander. The house, second from the left on Harbour Road (the one that has been built with the gable showing), was John Watt the boatbuilder's house. John Watt & Sons, boatbuilders, was founded in Gardenstown in 1940. The firm had a yard on the Newground where they built a large range of clinker lifeboats and motor boats. They acquired the yard of Stephen's of Banff in 1955 and in 1966 they bought the building yard and engineering facilities of Macduff Engineering Co. The name of the yard was changed to Macduff Boatbuilding & Engineering Co. and the company finally became Macduff Shipyards Ltd in 1985. The area to the east, left of the harbour, was made up mainly of warehouses and industrial buildings. The warehouse on the far left of the photograph is one of many; on the upper level there were individual net stores for keeping and mending nets and, on the lower level, was the coal merchant's store. At the beginning of the twentieth century the coal merchant was Jock Craigen. Fully laden coal boats would have had to wait until the tide was high enough to allow them to enter the harbour. There were only two lorries in the village at this time so Mr Craigen would hire farmers with horses and carts to help to unload and transport the coal from the west pier around the harbour to the store.

Alec Fraser Watt, sitting on the east pier watching over his uncle John George West's boat, the *Silver Spray*. During the 1970s this image was printed onto tea sets, which were then sold in a shop in the village. The small wooden shed below the church was the Coastguard's watch hut. The broad quay on the left was designed to accommodate the gutting and curing of the herring that was landed. During the boom herring fishing years of the late 1800s and early 1900s, villages like Gardenstown provided the industry with thousands of skilled gutting girls, known locally as 'gutting quines', who would gut and pack the herring into barrels. As the herring migrated around the coast of Britain the gutting quines would follow.

All three of the boats in this picture are Fifies, although by this time they had been converted from sail to diesel power. The boat in the centre of the photograph is BF46 *Verbena*, owned by Garden Murray (Gairnie) who is on the left. In 1929 the lighting of the harbour was changed from paraffin lamps to acetylene gas. The old gas house can be seen on the pier on the right; its position is now taken by the public toilets.

The Harbour
Gardenstown

To the right of the slipway the sandy area was another favourite playground for the children of the village. The steps on the west pier were removed and replaced with ladders during the mid 1980s. Work had begun on replacing the Seatown road – you can see that the new road only reaches the bottom of Strait Path (to the right of the house next to the grass bank on the right of the harbour buildings). The boat at the front right is the *Chrissies*, owned by John Wiseman (Jocky Hittie). The boat with the tiny wheelhouse, second in from the harbour wall and nearest the middle of the harbour, is the *Wayfarer*, owned by brothers Willie and George Ritchie. As well as changes in the way the fishing boats were powered – from sail, to steam, to diesel – they were also getting bigger and so the harbour in Gardenstown was eventually unable to moor them. Many of the Gardenstown-owned boats were then moved to the larger, deeper harbours in nearby Banff, Macduff and Fraserburgh.

The three storey building next to the harbour office on the far right was Jock Craigen's Ship Chandlery shop. On the front left of the shop you can just make out the petrol pump. This building was later taken over by the fishermen's co-operative, the GFU (Gardenstown Fishermen's Union). The boat at the front of the photograph is the *Silver Spray*, owned by John George West. The concrete 'lang stair' from the Braehead, Main Street, down to Harbour Road replaced an earlier set of wooden steps. In 1913 work started on enlarging the harbour. The Harbour Trustees bought a narrow gauge railway to help transport stone from near the point of Mohr Head to beneath the old churchyard of St John's, and also from the Sneuk over the Newground to the stone crushing plant and traction engine which were located near the west pier. The train which ran around the Sneuk was named *Bosco*. The lighthouse at the end of the east pier was added in 1914 and work on the new west pier continued until about 1915 when, after a series of unfortunate events, the company employed to do the work went into receivership and the pier was never completed.

The curing yard at the Newground was set up every year on a temporary basis to help to keep up with the quantity of fish landed and the high demand from customers. Traditionally the women would work in teams of three: two gutters and a packer. Labourers would keep them supplied with fish, and coopers with barrels. The man on the far right is holding a wooden gauge used for grading the fish by size; any 'burst' or damaged fish would be sent to make fishmeal which was used for animal feedstuffs and sometimes fertiliser.

CHURCH ROAD GARDENSTOWN.

At the bottom left of this photograph can be seen part of the Cement Houses and the small stone building that was the toilet for all six houses! The rough ground up the brae behind these homes was used for drying washing and nets. Later on this area was divided up and used as allotments. When this photograph was taken in the early 1900s the white house on the right, No. 139 Church Road, was home to Andrew Davidson and his spinster sister, Polly. Above this house is the plain, gaunt United Free Presbyterian church which was built in 1875 as a 'chapel-of-ease' to spare the older villagers the walk out into the country to the Gamrie Parish Church. After the UF Church and the Church of Scotland reunited in the 1920s, the Brethren, who actually owned the building, began to use it as a meeting hall. By 1955 this meeting was so well attended that the hall was extended with a square flat roofed extension. It was used by the Brethren until the mid 1980s when it became a private residence, now known as High Green Hall. The Church of Scotland building to the left of the photograph was built in 1899. This church replaced an earlier one on this site which had been built in 1856. The horse and trap travelling up the road are believed to have belonged to the local doctor.

34

Looking down towards the Braehead from the top of Tullytowan; the original wooden stair from the Braehead down to the harbour can be seen lower right of centre. Mohr Head, the sea cliff to the west of the village, stands some 536 feet above sea level. The first shipwreck to be recorded off Gardenstown was that of the *Reliance* in 1803. This 198-ton vessel, carrying coal from North Shields to Jamaica, was wrecked at Mohr Head. Only one of the eleven crew was rescued, Colin Burns from Montrose.

HIGH GREEN, GARDENSTOWN.

The house on the right looking out over Crovie is Airylea Cottage. It was built sometime between 1901 and 1911 by John Steven, druggist (or pharmacist) who lived there with his wife Elspet and their two daughters, Mary and Hilda. The eldest, Mary, became a teacher at Bracoden Public School. The cottages on the left are older than Airylea. The top cottage on the road is Seaview Cottage which was actually divided into three separate houses, A, B and C. The 1901 census tells us that in A lived Francis Johnston, a tailor, with his wife Jane and their six children; in B lived spinster sisters Margaret and Jessie Johnston, along with a niece and nephew; and in C lived George Wilson, a widower, with his daughter, Lizzie Johnston. The cottage nearest the washing line is Rockmount.

The United Free manse, seen here around 1915, once stood on its own on the outskirts of the village; today it is the second house as you enter the village and the field surrounding it is now filled with modern bungalows. At one time this was the Church of Scotland manse, but it became a private dwelling after the UF Church reunited with the Church of Scotland in the late 1920s. It was bought by the Johnston family at this time.

THE MANSE GAMRIE.

The Rev. Patrick Thomas Clark, who was minister of the parish church from 1875 to 1915, is seen here standing in front of the manse around 1909. It was built around 1830, possibly by William Robertson of Elgin. The house is a fine example of Georgian architecture, with its symmetrical frontage, central entrance and bracketed cornice, panelled door and long ground floor windows. To the rear of the building there is a projecting bowed stairwell. A wing was added later in the 1800s to form an L-plan. The steading next to the manse is a single-storey, U-plan building which contained a byre, stables and coach house.

GAMRIE PARISH CHURCH.

The Rev. Patrick Thomas Clark standing in front of the 'new' parish church. Located approximately one mile inland from Gardenstown, this was built in 1829 by William Robertson of Elgin to replace the old Church of St John's. The first service held in the new church took place on 20 June 1829. The minister at the time was Thomas Wilson Jnr, AM, who was minister between 1818 and 1855. He was the son of the preceding Thomas Wilson, and the third generation of the Wilson family to be minister of the parish. He was also the writer of parish's entry in the *New Statistical Account of Scotland*, which was published in 1842 and recorded details of local society. This church is now a private residence, although the churchyard is still in use.

The Snook, Gardenstown.

From the Newground area of Gardenstown you can pick up the mile-long footpath known as the Sneuk (or Snook), which follows the bottom of the cliffs to Crovie. This allowed the residents of Crovie to easily access the shops and facilities of Gardenstown without having to resort to the very steep four-mile trip via the road. In the early 1900s a passageway was blasted through the rock of the Sneuk, which is the rocky outcrop jutting out seawards, allowing almost year round access, the only exceptions being during the very high spring tides and during stormy weather. After the Great Storm of 1953 the Sneuk path was all but washed away. The path was repaired, and indeed has been repaired a number of times since, and is still in use today.

CROVIE.

At the end of the fishing season smaller boats were pulled up the beach, past the high water mark, so that repair work and painting could be undertaken. Crovie's small harbour, seen here, was built in 1883 after three local fishermen drowned whilst trying to enter the 'creek', which is where the burn meets the sea at the top of the pier. A fourth survived by struggling onto rocks with the oars. In the late nineteenth century Crovie had its own fishing fleet of approximately sixty boats and around 100 fishermen. The fleet moved to Gardenstown after the damage caused by the storm in 1953.

Opposite: This picture of Crovie from around 1901 shows two sisters, Mary Helen and Jane Watt, watching fisherman Alexander Johnston baiting his lines for fishing outside his house (No. 6). To the left is a pile of nets on which cod is being dried. The man outside his house in the background (No. 8) is George Watt (Peter), who was well known locally for his fiddle playing. George's family were all musical; his direct descendant, Gavin Sutherland of The Sutherland Brothers, wrote the words and music of the song 'Sailing', which gave Rod Stewart a worldwide hit in the 1970s. When George's house was knocked down in 1958 (by then it was a ruin) 'Peter Johnston 1789' was found carved on the fireplace – Peter Johnston was the great uncle of Alexander seen here! Birth records in the Parish of Gamrie were started in 1704; the name Watt was most prominent in Crovie, with Watt, Wiseman and Nicol being well established in Gardenstown.

Above: In 1901 the population of Crovie was approximately 398. Ten years later it had fallen to 282 but there were fifty children from Crovie alone attending Bracoden School, almost as many as the entire school roll from the surrounding area today! After the storm in 1953 a lot of the Crovie families sold up and moved to Gardenstown. The village has around 65 cottages and now most of them are used as holiday homes which make an ideal refuge from modern life as there is no mobile phone reception at the bottom of the cliffs. Crovie is one of the few remaining places still to have a working red phone box. The steam ship *Vigilant* ran aground at Crovie during a storm on 11 February 1906; she was carrying coal from Sunderland to Inverness. The residents of Crovie went to their rescue, saving all the lives on board.

Opposite: A crowd watching children enjoy the very cold water in the swimming pool at Bracoden School. The pool, completed in 1959, was paid for by the people of Gardenstown. Every Friday the pupils would take a 'pool penny' to school to add to the collection. The pool was built by the pupils with the aid of the janitor. At science class on a Friday the boys made cement, which was poured into moulds and allowed to set. The cement blocks were then taken out of the moulds at science class on a Tuesday (made at a rate of twelve blocks at a time) until they had enough to build the pool. A roof was added in 1962. Today the pool remains in use, although now it is also heated!

The roadside hamlet of Protstonhill lies on the B9031 road between Crovie and Pennan. The building in the centre of the photograph with the two men standing nearby beside the cart was the local smiddy.

Troup House, Banffshire.

Troup House is located at the eastern end of the Parish of Gamrie. The original grim looking mansion of 1770 (see opposite page) was replaced in 1897 by the current house, seen here. It was designed and built by R.G. Wilson, an architect from Aberdeen. It is recorded that on 31 August 1746 Alexander Garden was kidnapped from Troup House by Jacobite rebels and held at ransom – he was released after one week without the ransom being paid. Four years later he planted around 700 acres of beech and Scots fir trees on the Tore of Troup and around Troup House. Today Troup House, part of the Priory Group, is a specialist day and residential school for young people who have emotional and social difficulties. Nearby Troup Head is now an RSPB reserve with the only mainland gannet colony in Scotland.

OLD TROUP HOUSE.

The beach at Cullykhan has always been a popular site for campers. By the end of the pier is the Needles Eye, a slit of a cave through which you can enter a larger cave known as the Devil's Dining Room. The area to the left of the beach is a real historical and geological hotspot: by following a narrow footpath you can reach the site of an ancient hill fort, Fort Fiddes. The site has been found to contain evidence of a Bronze Age settlement and later was under Pictish and Roman occupation. There was also a medieval stronghold here. From this site you can see the opening at the top of Hell's Lum, through which sea spray shoots out like a column of smoke during storms. Local folklore claims that there is a smuggler's tunnel leading from the Devil's Dining Room to Troup House.

TORE OF TROUP GAMRIE.

It's believed that this house at the Tore of Troup is the original Troup House, which was home to Alexander Garden, founder of Gardenstown. It is an eighteenth century single-storey building with long elevations to the north and south. The east end of the building was formerly the threshing barn with a kiln, while the west end was the cart shed. The 'tore', from which the farm takes its name, is a deep and lengthy valley which cuts inland for approximately three miles towards the Hill of Troup. Halfway along the valley there is a holy well and the site of a pre-Reformation chapel. The valley there marked the boundary between the old counties of Aberdeen and Banff.

The area around Cullykhan near Pennan is full of hidden bays, caves and dramatic cliffs. These would have made an ideal haven for smugglers; although fishing was the main industry of Pennan, smuggling came a close second with the main contraband being silk and liquor. The village of Pennan was established by the seventeenth century and in the past it has been known as St Magnus Haven and Auchmeddan. It is located in the Parish of Aberdour, to the east of Gardenstown from which it is separated by Troup Head (396 feet). The building halfway up the hill above the village, with the flag pole in the garden, is the coastguard's house.

The Pennan Church, officially the Auchmeddan Mission Church, in the top left of this photograph, was built in 1884. Up until 1883 the people of Pennan had been travelling three miles over steep hills to Aberdour to attend church. The villagers wanted a church of their own and, under the guidance of the Rev. James Wilson, a fund was begun which was to finance the building of one. The village had a wealth of craftsmen including boatbuilders, carpenters, stonemasons and quarrymen who all gave freely their time, skills and labour to help with the construction. Red sandstone blocks from the quarries on the west of Red Head were hauled up Pennan Brae by teams of Clydesdale horses and smaller stones were carried up the hill by the women of the village in creels carried on their backs. Unfortunately, Mr Wilson died in August 1883 and never saw the finished church. The building next to it is the schoolhouse and the building with the flag flying is the coastguard's house.

In 1835 the population of Pennan was 180 and by 1900 it had increased to over 300. By that time the village was booming and, as well as a herring curer, the village had at least three shipwrights, three shoemakers, a tailor, an inn, a baker, a butcher, a grocer, a transport contractor, a blacksmith, and also banking services. The improvements in fishing technology had a detrimental effect on the village; as the boats outgrew the harbour they were moored elsewhere and slowly the population followed, as did the amenities. The area above the village, behind the four cottages at the top of the photograph, was divided up into allotments where the villagers grew fresh vegetables. Today Pennan is one of the most visited villages along the Banffshire coast. The village and its infamous red phone box found fame as the key location of the 1983 film *Local Hero*.

RED HEAD, PENNAN.

Pennan is sheltered between Troup Head to the west and Red Head to the east. The village was well known in the nineteenth century for the millstones that were quarried to the east of the village, and which were shipped out from the harbour or simply rolled on their edge to more local destinations. Rolling a millstone up the hill behind the village must have been a challenge but stones taken from this quarry were said to be the best in Britain. At the east end of Pennan lies its harbour. These days it is still used by a couple of fishing vessels, but otherwise its life revolves around leisure craft. The first harbour at the village was built in 1704, but by the end of the century it had fallen into disuse and a replacement was built in 1799. By 1840 this harbour too was no longer usable, and a bigger and better one was built in 1845. This third harbour lasted until a storm in the winter of 1889/90 destroyed the west pier, which was replaced in 1903. The harbour was further improved in 1909 and again in 1981.

PENNAN NEAR FRASERBURGH

52765

As at Crovie, the boats of Pennan were drawn up on the shingle beach at the end of the fishing season so that repair work and painting could take place. The coastguard's house is just visible over the top of the cliff; a viewing platform with a rail stands just in front of it.

A photograph of the west end of Pennan, possibly taken on the day of King George V's coronation on 6 May 1910 which would explain the finery of the women's clothes.

Further Reading

The books listed below were used by the author during her research. None of them are available from Stenlake Publishing. Those interested in finding out more are advised to contact their local bookshop or reference library.

Entries for the parishes of Gamrie and Aberdour in the *Statistical Account of Scotland* of 1791–99 and 1834–45, and the county of Banff in the *Statistical Account of Scotland* of 1961

Auchmeddan Church Centenary Magazine, 1884–1974

Gavin Bell, *The Kirkyard of St John's, Parish of Gamrie*, 2006

HB, RC, AG, JP, AWW, HGW (full names not given), *A' tween Troup Heid & Gamrie Mohr*, 1968

Francis H. Groome, *Ordnance Gazetteer of Scotland: A Survey of Scottish Topography, Statistical, Biographical and Historical*, 1882–85

Ed Knipe, *Gamrie: An Exploration in Cultural Ecology*, 1984

Allan Edward Mahood, *Banff and District*, 1919

Joe Reid, *Steam Drifters Recalled: Whitehills to St Combs*, 2001

Rosemary Sanderson, *The Herring Lassies: Following The Herring*, 2008

Nigel Tranter, *The Queen's Scotland: The North East*, 1974

Websites

Aberdeenshire Council Sites & Monuments Records: http://www.aberdeenshire.gov.uk/smrpub/shire/default.aspx
British Listed Buildings Online: www.britishlistedbuildings.co.uk
Royal Commission on the Ancient and Historical Monuments of Scotland: www.rcahms.gov.uk
Gamrie Business Forum – Discover Gardenstown: www.discovergardenstown.co.uk
SCRAN: www.scran.ac.uk